CHILDREN'S ENCYCLOPEDIA

THE WORLD OF KNOWLEDGE

SCIENTISTS

Manasvi Vohra

V&S PUBLISHERS

Published by:

V&S PUBLISHERS

F-2/16, Ansari road, Daryaganj, New Delhi-110002
☎ 23240026, 23240027 • *Fax:* 011-23240028
Email: info@vspublishers.com • *Website:* www.vspublishers.com

Regional Office : Hyderabad
5-1-707/1, Brij Bhawan (Beside Central Bank of India Lane)
Bank Street, Koti, Hyderabad - 500 095
☎ 040-24737290
E-mail: vspublishershyd@gmail.com

Branch Office : Mumbai
Jaywant Industrial Estate, 2nd Floor-222, Tardeo Road
Opposite Sobo Central, Mumbai - 400 034
☎ 022-23510736
E-mail: vspublishersmum@gmail.com

Follow us on:

All books available at **www.vspublishers.com**

Printed at : Repro Knowledgecast Limited, Thane

PUBLISHER'S NOTE

V&S Publishers is glad to announce the launch of a unique, set of 12 books under the head, *Children's Encyclopedia – The World of Knowledge.* The set of 12 books namely – *Physices, Chemistry, Space Science, General Sceince, Life Science, Human Body, Electronics & Communications, Scientists, Inventions & Discoveries, Transportation, The Earth, and GK (General Knowledge)* has been especially developed keeping in mind the students and children of all age groups, particularly from 6 to 14 years of age. Our main aim is to arouse the interest and solve the queries of the school children regarding the various and diverse topics of Science and help them master the subject thoroughly.

In the book, *Scientists,* the author has broadly dealt with some world renowned and famous Scientists such as *Archimedes, Alexander Graham Bell, Albert Einstein, Benjamin Franklin, Charles Robert Darwin, Galileo Galilei, George Eastman, Sir Isaac Newton, Louis Pasteur, Michael Faraday, Marie Curie,* etc.

Each chapter is followed by a section called **Quick Facts** that contains a set of interesting and fascinating facts about the topics already discussed in the chapter. At the end of the book there is **Glossary** of difficult words and scientific terms to make the book complete and comprehensive.

Quick Facts

❦ Galileo Galilei taught geometry, mechanics and astronomy at the University of Padua from 1592 to 1610.

Though our aim is to be flawless, but errors might have crept in inadvertently. So we request our esteemed readers to read the book thoroughly and offer valuable suggestions wherever necessary to improve and enhance the quality of the book. Hope it interests you all and serves its purpose well.

CONTENTS

SCIENTISTS

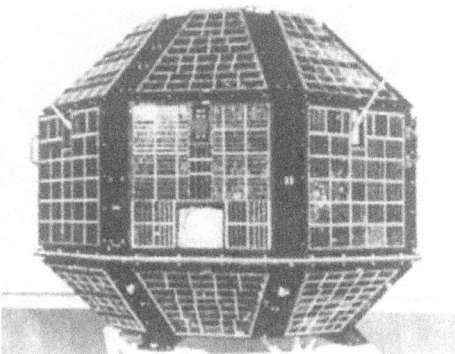

SCIENTISTS

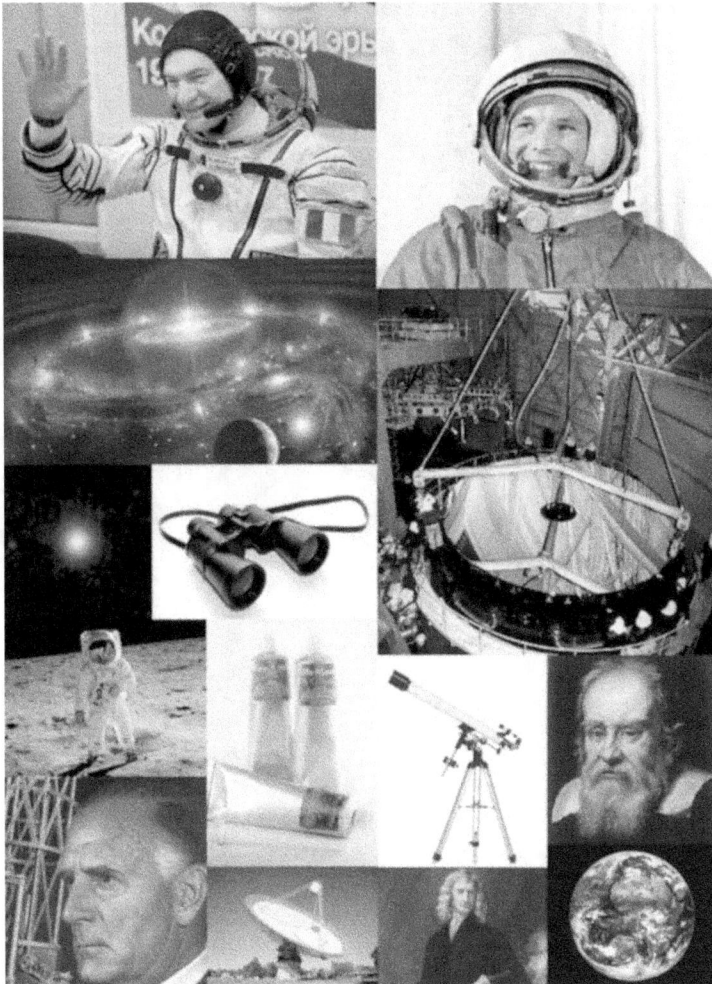

Chapter - 1

ARCHIMEDES
(287 BC–212 BC)

Biography

Archimedes was a Greek mathematician, physicist, astronomer, engineer and inventor. He is famous for giving what is today known as 'Archimedes Principle' among his other works. He was also famous for Archimedes' screw, hydrostatics, levers and infinitesimals.

Archimedes was born in the ancient city of Syracuse, Sicily in C 287 BC.

Did You Know?

Archimedes was asked by *King Hieron II* to test a gold crown of its purity without melting the crown. Archimedes was getting into his bathtub thinking over the question when he noticed the water level rising. He ran out crying 'Eureka' on the streets but without his clothes!

Archimedes Principle

Archimedes stated that whenever a solid object is wholly or partially immersed in water, it experiences an upward force by water. This force is called the 'Buoyant' force which displaces certain amount of water. The amount of the water displaced is equal to the volume of that object.

You must have seen very heavy logs of wood floating through rivers or boats and ships moving on water. Logs of wood float on water because of the Archimedes Principle of buoyancy. Same is the case with boats and ships. A boat keeps floating because water gives it an upward push. The heavier the load gets on the boat, the water pushes it upward with more force. But if the water comes up to the level of the boat's edge, there would be no more upward push and the boat will sink.

Archimedes has many inventions and discoveries to his credit. He contributed in the field of *mathematics, science and defence.* Following are some of his works:

- **Archimedes Screw:** This was used to lift water from a low-lying water body to a certain height.

Archimedes Screw

- **Claw of Archimedes:** The Claw of Archimedes is a weapon that he is said to have designed in order to defend the city of Syracuse. Also known as "the ship shaker," the claw consisted of a crane-like arm from which a large metal grappling hook was suspended.

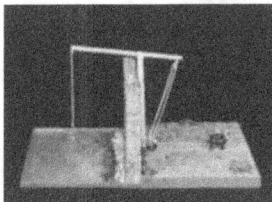
Archimedes Clan

When the claw was dropped onto an attacking ship the arm would swing upwards, lifting the ship out of the water and possibly sinking it. There have been modern experiments to test the feasibility of the claw, and in 2005, a television documentary entitled Superweapons of the

Ancient World built a version of the claw and concluded that it was a workable device.

- ☀ **Value of Pie:** It is a very significant discovery in the field of Mathematics. Archimedes shows that the value of pi (π) is greater than 223/71 and less than **22/7**. The latter figure was used as an approximation of pi throughout the Middle Ages and is still used today when only a rough figure is required.

- ☀ **On the Equilibrium of Planes (two volumes):** The first book is in 15 propositions with seven postulates, while the second book is in ten propositions. In this work, Archimedes explains the Law of the Lever, stating, "Magnitudes are in equilibrium at distances reciprocally proportional to their weights." Archimedes uses the principles derived to calculate the areas and centres of gravity of various geometric figures including *triangles, parallelograms and parabolas.*

- ☀ **Archimedes Heat Rays:** Mirrors were placed at different angles on seashores so that they all of them reflect the sunrays at a single point, usually on an enemy ship during the war. The amount of sun's heat would be so high that it would burn the ship.

Archimedes Heat Rays

✩ Archimedes was able to use infinitesimals in a way that is similar to the modern integral calculus. This technique is known as the method of exhaustion, and he employed it to the approximate the value of π which is approximately **3.1416**. He also proved that the area of a circle was equal to π multiplied by the square of the radius of the circle (πr^2).

On the Sphere and Cylinder, Archimedes postulates that any magnitude when added to itself enough times will exceed any given magnitude. This is the Archimedean property of real numbers.

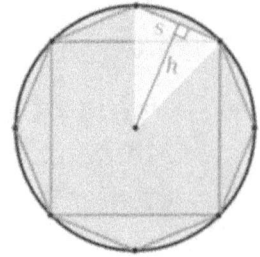

Archimedes was killed by the Roman soldiers when collaborators let the Romans into Syracuse in 212 BC.

Quick Facts

- Archimedes was one of the greatest scientists who created the sciences of mechanics and hydrostatics.

- Archimedes was a Greek who lived in the city of Syracuse, Sicily. His relative, Hieron II, was the king of Syracuse.

- To help defend Syracuse against Roman attackers in 215BC, Archimedes invented many war machines. They included an awesome 'claw' — a giant grappling crane that could lift whole galleys from the water and sink them.

- He stated that the volume of an object is the amount of surface occupied by it. He also discovered that objects float because they are thrust upwards by the water.

- Archimedes analysed levers mathematically. He showed that the load you can move with a particular effort is in exact proportion to its distance from the fulcrum.

Chapter - 2

ALEXANDER GRAHAM BELL
(1847–1922)

Alexander Graham Bell is one of the pioneering inventors of the modern age. Born in *Edinburgh, Scotland* on March 3, 1847, Bell was a scientist, inventor, engineer and innovator. He invented the first **'Telephone'**.

Biography

Alexander went to the *University of Edinburgh* and later to the *University of London*. Bell was a remarkable child and at a very young age of 12, he made his first invention – a wheat dehusking machine fitted with a set of paddles and nail brushes.

Discoveries and Inventions

Since a very young age, he was involved in devising ways to help the deaf-mute people communicate. He devised hearing instruments for the deaf people and based on these, he progressed to the invention of telephone. *He established a school*

A Wheat Husking Machine

for the deaf and mutes in Boston, Massachusetts in 1872. He made his first telephone on June 2, 1875 and at the age of 29, Bell presented his first 'telephone' to the world in the year 1876. In 1877, he formed the Bell Telephone Company.

Bell's Telephone

Did You Know?

Thomas A. Watson, an engineer, was Bell's assistant. The first words, Bell spoke on the telephone were directed to him- "Mr. Watson, come here. I want to see you."

After the invention of telephone, Bell invented a 'photophone' – a device that enabled sound to be transmitted through a beam of light. This device was made from a sensitive selenium crystal and a mirror that vibrated in response to a sound. Bell regarded this invention as his greatest, even greater than the telephone. Today's fibre, laser and optics communication systems are based on the *principles of Alexander Graham Bell's photophone.*

Bell was engaged in a wide variety of scientific researches and inventions like aeroplanes, telecommunication, artificial respiration, etc.

Bell's Photophone

Bell is also credited with the invention of the metal detector in 1881. The device was quickly put together in an attempt to find the bullet in the body of US President James Garfield. The metal detector worked flawlessly in tests but did not find the assassin's bullet partly because the metal bed frame on which the President was lying disturbed the instrument, resulting in static.

In 1891, Bell had begun experiments to develop the motor-powered heavier-than-air, aircraft. The AEA was first formed as Bell shared the vision to fly with his wife, who advised him to seek "young" help as Alexander was 60 years old.

In 1898, Bell experimented with tetrahedral box kites and wings constructed of multiple compound tetrahedral kites covered in maroon silk. The tetrahedral wings were named Cygnet I, II and III, and were flown both

Bell's Metal Detector

unmanned and manned (Cygnet I crashed during a flight carrying Selfridge) in the period from 1907–1912. Some of Bell's kites are on display at the Alexander Graham Bell National Historic Site.

Alexander Graham Bell died on August 2, 1922 due to diabetic complications.

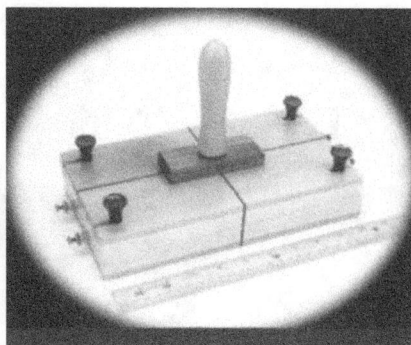

Quick Facts

- Alexander Graham Bell's first vocation was that of a teacher of the Deaf. Not only did Bell follow in his father's footsteps (the elder Bell's work in Visible Speech for the Deaf inspired Shaw's Pygmalion), but Bell's mother and wife were also deaf!

- Graham Bell's two brothers, Melville and Edward died at a very young age of the deadly disease, Tuberculosis.

- Alexander Graham Bell was an American inventor but a Scottish by birth.

- In the United States he began teaching the deaf-mutes, publicising the system called visible speech. He also became a naturalised U.S. citizen in 1882.

- In 1880, France bestowed on Bell the Volta Prize, worth 50,000 francs, for his remarkable invention of the Telephone. He used the money in founding the Volta Laboratory in Washington, D.C. and invented the photophone with his associates.

- Bell's other inventions include the audiometer, the induction balance, and the first wax recording cylinder, introduced in 1886.

- Bell was one of the co-founders of the National Geographic Society, and he served as its president from 1896 to 1904.

- He also helped to establish the journal, Science by financing it from 1883-1894.

Chapter - 3

ALBERT EINSTEIN
(1879–1955)

Albert Einstein is one of the best known scientists of modern age. A *German* by origin, Einstein was born on March 14, 1879. He is famous for his *'Theory of Relativity'* giving the very famous equation $E = mc^2$. He was conferred the **Nobel Prize** for his contribution in the field of Physics. He is said to be the **Father of Modern Physics**.

Biography

Albert Einstein was born at *Ulm, in Württemberg, Germany*. He did his basic schooling from Luitpold Gymnasium, Munich. Einstein obtained his doctor's degree in 1905 and in 1914, and was appointed as a Professor of the University of Berlin. He received a *Nobel Prize* in Physics in the year, 1921. In 1933, Einstein migrated to America as a Professor of Theoretical Physics at Princeton and became a US citizen in 1940.

Did You Know?

Einstein once remarked, "A question that sometimes drives me crazy: am I or the others are crazy?"

Discoveries and Inventions

Albert Einstein's most salient work, for which he is justly famous for, is the Theory of relativity which was published in 1916. It states that the energy possessed by an object depends upon the mass of that object.

$E = mc^2$ where, E = energy, m = mass of the object, c = the speed of light

The more the mass of the object, the more the amount of energy it has.

He also worked to shed light on the many areas of Physics and found the basis of some important revelations on which works like *Quantum Physics, Photoelectric Effect and Brownian Motion* are based.

Some of Einstein's important and well-known scholarly works are the *Special Theory of Relativity* (1905), *Relativity* (English translations, 1920 and 1950), *General Theory of Relativity* (1916), *Investigations on the Theory of Brownian Movement* (1926), and *The Evolution of Physics* (1938).

About Zionism (1930), *Why War?* (1933), *My Philosophy* (1934), and *Out of My Later Years* (1950) are perhaps some of his most popular non-scientific works.

Einstein died on April 18, 1955 due to internal bleeding. He worked until the very end of his life, such was his genius.

Quick Facts

- Einstein was actually born with an abnormally large head, which doctors were concerned could be a sign that he was mentally retarded.

- He was later awarded the Nobel Prize for his work on the photo-electric effect.

- In 1895, at the age of 17, Albert Einstein applied for early admission into the Swiss Federal Polytechnical School (Eidgenössische Technische Hochschule or ETH). He passed the math and science sections of the entrance exam, but failed the rest, i.e., (history, languages, geography, etc.)!

Chapter - 4

BENJAMIN FRANKLIN
(1706–1790)

Benjamin Franklin was a celebrated American scientist, politician and author. He is regarded as one of the founding fathers of the United States. He was also the first United States Ambassador to France.

Biography

Benjamin Franklin was born on January 17, 1706 in Boston, Massachusetts. He did his schooling from Boston Latin School. Benjamin started working in his brother's newspaper as an apprentice. Later on in his life, he proved to be a successful newspaper editor and printer. He was the first to build a public library in America and a fire station in Pennsylvania. Benjamin ventured in many businesses, but is remembered mainly as a scientist.

Did You Know?

Benjamin Franklin never got a patent against his inventions as he believed that his work is for public welfare and not to gain profit.

Discoveries and Inventions

Franklin has many discoveries and inventions to his credit. He was the one to discover the 'principle of conservation of energy'. After his famous experiment with an iron key attached to a kite, he concluded that buildings could be saved from striking lightning (electric charge from the clouds) by placing a sharp pointed iron rod on the topmost part of the building, which goes all the way under the earth. This way, the electric charge would pass through the rod to the earth without affecting the building. He invented the 'lightning rod' for this purpose, which are used all over the world now. He was the one to name opposite charges of electricity as 'positive' and 'negative'.

Did You Know?

Benjamin Franklin *invented a tool* - long arm – a wooden rod with a clawing hand to reach to the books kept on high shelves.

Franklin also gave the world, *'bifocals'* – spectacles with two lenses in each frame so that a person could use the same spectacle for watching near and far things at the same time. Among his other inventions are Franklin stove, glass armonica and odometer.

Benjamin Franklin died on April 17, 1790 in Philadelphia.

Quick Facts

- Benjamin Franklin was the ninth child out of eleven children. His father was Josiah a candle/soap maker.

- When he was 16, he became a vegetarian so he could spend his money on books instead of meat. He was the first mailman in Philadelphia.

- He was a civil worker, inventor, a founding father, scientist, publisher and author, and held many political positions such as Minister to France which caused frequent travel to other countries.

- He was the only person to sign the Constitution, Declaration of Independence, and the Treaty of Paris of 1776.

- Benjamin Franklin was at the age of seventy when he signed the Declaration of Independence.

Chapter - 5

CHARLES ROBERT DARWIN
(1809–1882)

Charles Robert Darwin was an *English scientist and naturalist*. He is famously remembered for his scientific theory of evolution named as *'Natural Selection'*.

Biography

Charles Robert Darwin was born on February 12, 1809 in Shrewsbury, Shorpshire, England in a wealthy family. He was the fifth child. Darwin graduated from the elite school of Shrewsbury in 1825. After that, he enrolled in the University of Edinburgh to study medicine. But in 1827, he dropped out of Edinburgh and got admitted to the University of Cambridge. On completing his graduation in 1831, a 22-year-old Darwin embarked on a journey of scientific exploration as a naturalist around the world.

Discoveries and Inventions

After returning back from his expedition in 1836, Darwin started recording his views and ideas on the evolution process of the earth, based on the things he had observed during his voyage. By 1838, he had a rough sketch of his theory of evolution through natural selection. This theory was first announced in 1858.

The Theory of Evolution through Natural Selection states that an individual born in any species has to compete with its surrounding for its survival. The cycle goes on like this and that particular species evolve along with some variations depending upon its surroundings. These variations are passed on to the next generation through heredity, thus marking the evolution of the species.

Evolution of Man

Did You Know?

The Theory of Evolution through Natural Selection gave the phrase, 'Survival of the fittest'.

Darwin also observed that all related organisms are evolved from common ancestors. He also mentioned that the earth is an evolving entity and not static in nature.

Darwin's Theory of Evolution met with criticism from his fraternity. Fellow scientists criticised him saying that he can't prove his theory. Others challenged him to prove his theory of origin of variation in species and how it is possible to pass those variations to the next generation.

Charles Robert Darwin died on April 19, 1882 in his home near London.

- February 12, 1809, was a very significant day in history. Not only was Charles Darwin born that day, the famous President of the United States, Abraham Lincoln was also born that day.

- Charles Darwin is often called the "Father of Evolution".

- Darwin attended the Edinburgh University in hopes of becoming a physician like his father, but soon abandoned the idea because he couldn't stand the sight of blood.

- Charles Darwin was quite sick in his later years. He is believed to have caught Chagas Disease while in South America. This disease is caused by the bite of of a certain bug.

- Even though Charles Darwin was not a Buddhist himself, he and his wife Emma had an alleged fascination of and respect for the religion. Darwin wrote a book called Expressions of the Emotions in Man and Animals in which he explained that compassion in humans was a trait that survived natural selection because it is a beneficial trait to want to stop the suffering of others.

Chapter - 6

GALILEO GALILEI
(1564–1642)

Galileo was an Italian mathematician, astronomer, physicist and philosopher. He is famously remembered for the Galilean Telescope and his observations of the universe.

Biography

Galileo was born on February 15, 1564 in Pisa, Italy. His father was a musician and wool trader. He wanted his son to study medicine. Galileo began his education in Jesuit monastery at the age of 11. By the time he was 17, he was enrolled with the University of Pisa to learn medicine.

In university, mathematics became his favourite subject, so much so that he shunned other subjects and began studying only maths. Later, to earn his living, he began taking maths tuitions for other students.

Did You Know?

Galileo wanted to be a monk when he came back from the Jesuit monastery. His father got angry and withdrew him from there.

Discoveries and Inventions

At the age of 21, he discovered the 'law of pendulum'. He saw a lamp swing to and fro from the ceiling of a church. He then timed the swinging of the lamp with his pulse and to his astonishment, found that each swing was completed in equal time. This formed the basis of the law of pendulum. He invented the military compass.

But his most important invention was the Galilean telescope. He started with a 3-power telescope and later refined it to 10- power. It was through this telescope that he noticed that the moon has craters and that planets revolve around the sun. This observation made him support the heliocentric theory stated by **Nicolaus Copernicus**. *This theory states that the Sun is a stationary star and is at the centre of the Solar System. The Earth revolves around it and not the other way round.*

Galileo also challenged Aristotle's theory which states heavy objects fall at a greater speed during a free fall. Galileo dropped balls of different masses and sizes at the same time from the top of the Tower

Galilean Telescope

of Pisa. All the balls hit the ground at the same time. Galileo then stated that time taken by a free falling object to reach the ground is independent of its mass.

Galileo Galilei died on March 8, 1642 following a prolonged illness.

Quick Facts

- Galileo Galilei taught geometry, mechanics and astronomy at the University of Padua from 1592 to 1610.

- Galileo built his first telescope in 1609, which featured three times magnification. Later, he developed models that could see up to 30 times magnification.

- Galileo was a well-known and accomplished musician.

- He published his first astronomical observations in 1610. The collection was called "Starry Messenger."

- Galileo also was one of the first people to observe sunspots, which helped develop the predictions that would help identify the annual patterns.

- Using his telescopes, he was able to identify that the Moon had mountains and craters, dispelling the belief that it was a perfect sphere.

- Later in his life, Galileo became blind.

Chapter - 7

GEORGE EASTMAN
(1854–1932)

George Eastman was an *American inventor, entrepreneur* and a *philanthropist*. He is remembered for his invention of **film roll**. He was the founder of *Eastman Kodak Company*.

Quick Learn

A philanthropist is a person who spends money on humanity and social work.

Biography

George Eastman was born on July 12, 1854 in Waterville, New York. At the age of eight years, he started attending a private school in Rochester. After his father's death in 1862, Eastman's family condition became poor and he left his studies to earn money.

Eastman's Film Roll

Discoveries and Inventions

Eastman patented his first film roll in the year

1884. This was the first film roll to be proven practical as it was a dry, transparent, and flexible, photographic film. With the advent of film roll, there came a pioneering change in the field of photography.

In 1888, Eastman invented the Kodak camera. It was the first camera designed especially for the film roll.

Eastman's Kodak Camera

His aim was to simplify photography so that even masses could do photography.

Did You Know?

"You press the button, we do the rest" was the advertising slogan for Eastman's Kodak Camera.

George Eastman founded the Eastman Kodak Company in Rochester, New York in the year 1892. This company mass produced good quality photography equipments as well as the film roll invented by Eastman. It was the first of its kind photography company. The Kodak camera came with the pre-loaded film roll with 100 exposures. A person could use the camera and after finishing his role, could hand it back to the company. The company then removed the film roll, developed the photographs and inserted a new film roll before handing back the camera. Eastman's commercial, transparent film roll formed the basis of Thomas Edison's motion picture camera.

Apart from photographic revolution, Eastman is also fondly remembered for his charitable work. He donated money for the building of educational and health institutes. He donated to the Massachusetts Institute of Technology and also contributed for the establishment of the Eastman School of Music in 1918 and a school of medicine and dentistry in 1921 at the University of Rochester.

George Eastman died of gunshot on March 14, 1932.

- George Eastman was the first person to make the handheld Kodak camera.

- George Eastman's life in photography spans the half-century from 1880 to 1930, when science, technology and culture converged to create "new products" of all sorts.

- Eastman had built a "Method and Apparatus for Coating Plates" which made dry film a reality.

- In his final two years, Eastman was in intense pain, caused by a degenerative disorder affecting his spine.

Chapter - 8

SIR ISAAC NEWTON
(1642–1727)

Sir Isaac Newton was an English astronomer, physicist, philosopher and mathematician. He is regarded as the greatest scientist ever. He is famous for his laws of motion and the concept of gravitation.

Biography

Sir Isaac Newton was born on December 25, 1642 in Lincolnshire, England. Newton was named after his father – Isaac Newton, who died three months before his birth. He was a premature child and was raised by his maternal grandmother. Newton went to The King's School, Grantham when he turned 12. In 1661, he enrolled with the Trinity College, Cambridge. He obtained his degree in 1665. Later, he joined the same college as a mathematics professor.

Newton was knighted by Queen Anne in London in 1705 for his contribution in the field of science.

Why was 'Sir' added before a name?

Being knighted means to have the title, 'Sir' before one's name. Therefore, some scientists had 'Sir' before their names.

Discoveries and Inventions

Newton's law of gravity – Newton stated that every object in the universe experiences a pull towards every other object. This amount of pull or force depends upon the masses of the objects and the distance between them.

Did You Know?

Newton was sitting under an apple tree when an apple fell down from the tree and hit him on the head. This made him wonder why the apple fell down instead of falling in any other direction. And this is how the law of gravity came into light.

Newton gave three laws of motion. They are:

Gravitational Force

- ☄ **First Law:** It states that a stationary object will remain in rest until an external force puts it in motion and an object in motion will continue to be in uniform motion (same speed and same direction) until an external force acts upon it to change the speed or the direction. This is also called as the Inertia of Rest or the Inertia of Motion.

- ☄ **Second Law:** It states that more the mass of the object, the more is the force required to move that object.

- **Third Law:** It states that every action has an equal and opposite reaction.

Newton's laws of motion are the basis of some of the most advanced techniques and technologies in use today. These were first published in **1687**, titled **Principia**. Apart from these, he also proposed the Newton's theory of colour. He also did some important work in optics.

Sir Isaac Newton died on March 31, 1727 during his sleep.

Quick Facts

- Newton chose to live a life of celibacy, and he never married.
- Newton was always interested in how things worked. As a young boy at Woolsthorpe, Newton constructed sundials accurate within fifteen minutes.
- Newton also invented the Calculus and explained the visible spectrum of light.

Chapter - 9

LOUIS PASTEUR
(1822–1895)

Louis Pasteur was a French chemist and microbiologist. He is known for his significant contribution towards microbiology and is often regarded as one of the three founders of the subject. He created the first vaccines for rabies and anthrax.

Biography

Louis Pasteur was born in a tanner family on December 27, 1822 in Dole, France. He was a degree holder in mathematical sciences and joined the École Normale Supérieure College for higher studies. In 1848, he joined Dijon Lycée as a physics professor and later the University of Strasbourg as a professor of chemistry.

Pasteur had five children but only two of them survived. The other three died of typhoid. This personal grief led Pasteur to find about the cures to such life threatening diseases.

Discoveries and Inventions

Louis Pasteur was the first to observe that day to day processes, like souring of beer, wine and milk, happen because of micro-organisms present in our atmosphere. After a series of experiments and observations, he found out that if we heat these affected liquids, then we can successfully remove

Sour Milk

these micro organisms (germs). This process of heating liquids to remove harmful micro organisms is known as **pasteurisation**.

Louis Pasteur also mentioned that not only these germs affect things like wine, beer, milk, etc but also affect human beings and cause certain diseases. He studied the chickens suffering from chicken cholera and observed that if a cure for this disease can be found, then cures for other diseases caused by micro organisms can also be found.

Did You Know?

Doctors and surgeons sanitize their hands and equipments before and after every surgery. This practice was encouraged by Louis Pasteur because of his study of germs.

He also found out about the immunisation in a living being. He explained that when a living being is attacked by the same germ second time, his/ her body develops some amount of resistance towards the effects of that germ. This way, the germ is not able to cause serious infection to the living being. This resistance is known as the immune power of that living being.

Based on this immune power, Pasteur created vaccines for anthrax and rabies.

- In the honour of his work and influential contributions, Louis Pasteur was made a Grand Croix of the Legion of Honour, a prestigious French order.

- He is well known for inventing a process to stop food and liquid, such as milk from making people sick. This method is called Pasteurisation. It helps reduce the number of micro-organisms that could cause diseases while not affecting the quality and taste in a way which sterilization would.

- Micro-organisms are very tiny organisms that harm living beings by attacking any weak spot in their bodies. The harmful ones are called germs like different types of bacteria and viruses.

- Many of Pasteur's experiments supported the germ theory of disease, and they helped show that micro-organisms are the true cause of many diseases. In earlier times, people believed that diseases were spontaneously generated. However, over time this theory was superseded-- thanks to the work of Pasteur and many others.

Chapter - 10

MICHAEL FARADAY
(1791–1867)

Michael Faraday was an English physicist famous for his contribution in the field of physics and chemistry. The SI unit of capacitance is named 'Farad' to honour his contribution in the field of electromagnetism.

Biography

Michael Faraday was born on September 22, 1791 in Hampshire, England into a poor family. He was the third of four children and had very little basic education. When he was 14 years old, he became an apprentice with a local bookseller. It was here that he started reading books and found an inclination towards science. He started reading books on physics and chemistry and tried to apply the principles and suggestions of the books. Due to his correspondence with eminent scholars in these fields, he was appointed as a Chemical Assistant at the Royal Institution in 1813. This way he began the journey of his scientific exploration.

Did You Know?

Every Christmas, as a chemistry professor, Faraday used to give science lectures to a group of children from all age groups at the Royal Institution in London, England. These lectures grew very popular among the audiences and as a tradition, they are continued even today.

Discoveries and Inventions

Faraday is famous for his work on **electromagnets**. He was the one to state the **law of induction**. He observed that electricity could be generated by moving a piece

Faraday's Generator

of magnet continuously inside a metal wire coil. Based on this, he built the first basic electric motor, transformer and generator. His observations of electromagnetic induction led to the principles of converting mechanical energy into electrical energy.

Faraday is famous for laying the basis of the electric generator. Through this generator, one can convert mechanical energy to electrical energy.

He is also credited for discovering the laws of electrolysis. These laws and principles find applications in many industrial purposes like separating certain metals from their ores to obtain the pure metals. Similarly, batteries used in gadgets like remote controls, etc are based on electrolysis.

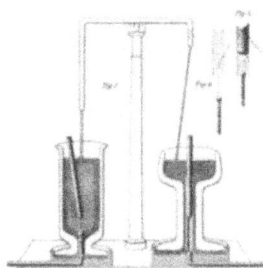

Electromagnetic Rotation

Faraday's Laws of Electrolysis

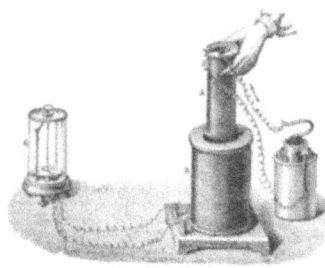

Induction Experiment

- Faraday was the son of a poor blacksmith, born in the village of Newington in Surrey, England.

- Until 1830, Faraday was mainly a chemist. In 1825, he discovered the important chemical, Benzene.

- Using his discovery of electric induction, Faraday made the first dynamo to generate electricity and so opened the way to the modern age of electricity.

Chapter - 11

MARIE CURIE
(1867–1934)

Marie Curie was a Polish physicist and chemist, known worldwide for her findings on radioactive substances. Often referred to as Madam Curie and Dr. Curie, she is the first person to win two Nobel Prizes – one in physics and the other in chemistry.

Biography

Marie Curie was born as Maria Salomea Skłodowska on November 7, 1867 in Warsaw, Kingdom of Poland to teacher parents. Curie worked as a governess for two years, assisting her sister to complete her college education. In the year 1890, she joined a laboratory at the Museum of Industry and Agriculture to begin her practical scientific training. In 1891, Marie left for France to join her sister and enrolled with the Sorbonne (University of Paris) to study, physics, chemistry and mathematics.

Discoveries and Inventions

Madam Curie observed that uranium emitted rays similar to X-rays and some harmful properties of these rays were indeed helpful to

eradicate tumour. She along with her husband, Pierre Curie, discovered two new radioactive elements 'polonium' and 'radium'. For this, they both were given the Nobel Prize in Physics, in the year 1901. These names were coined by both of them together – Polonium on Poland, the

Radium

birth land of Marie and Radium was named so because of his intense radioactivity. Even after her husband's death, she continued working on radioactive substances. In 1911, Marie Curie was honoured with a second Nobel Prize in Chemistry for successfully isolating pure radium and determining radium's atomic weight.

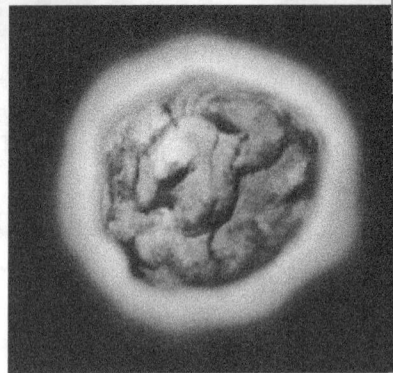

Did You Know?

Madam Curie was unaware of the dangers of radioactivity. She used to carry test tubes of radioactive substances in her coat pockets and stored them in her desk drawers. Her papers and books, kept in her laboratory – Musée Curie - are highly radioactive and are kept in protective boxes for the visitors to see.

Madam Curie died on July 4, 1934 in Poland due to constant exposure to the radioactive substances.

Quick Facts

- A radioactive substance is that which emits rays due to chemical reactions within its atoms. These substances are dangerous to handle without proper protection as they emit huge amount of rays, harmful for the body.

- Marie Curie was the first woman to win two Nobel Prizes in Science—both in Physics and Chemistry.

- Marie Curie fainted from hunger because she was so engrossed in her studies that she forgot to eat or drink properly for days together.

- She invented the term, radioactivity.

- She was proud of being Polish and named the first element she discovered after her homeland – Polonium.

Chapter - 12

THOMAS ALVA EDISON
(1847–1931)

Thomas Alva Edison or simply, Thomas Edison is the reason we have electric bulbs in our homes. He was an American inventor and businessman.

Biography

Thomas Edison was born on February 11, 1847 in Milan, Ohio as the seventh and last child to his parents, Samuel Ogden Edison and Nancy Matthews Elliott. He grew up in Port Huron, Michigan. He went to school for only three months and dropped out because he couldn't concentrate on his studies. He started doing little jobs like selling newspapers, candies and vegetables to supplement his chemical experiments. A few years later, he started a newspaper Grand Trunk Herald and with this, he started his career as a businessman. Edison had developed a hearing problem early in his life. However, this didn't deter him from continuing his research work.

Edison's Gifts

General Electric (GE), a successful multinational company was founded by Thomas Edison in 1890. You must have seen GE bulbs in the market. These are Edison's gifts to humanity.

Discoveries and Inventions

Edison's Electric Lamp

Edison began his career as an inventor in the year, **1877** with a **phonograph**. It is the basic version of the same device which we know as a **gramophone** and is used to play and record sounds.

In **1879**, Edison was able to produce a **light bulb**, using lower current electricity, a small carbonised filament and an improved vacuum inside the glass bulb. This bulb was a long-lasting and reliable source of electric light. After working on this experiment for one and a half years or more, Edison came up with an incandescent light bulb which was safe, economical and practical to use.

Edison's Light Bulb

Edison received his first patent on an electric vote recorder, a device intended for use by elected bodies to speed the voting process.

Edison's Phonograph

Did You Know?

Thomas Edison holds a record of having 1093 patents against his name in America alone. He also has many patents in United Kingdom, France and Germany.

Thomas Edison died on October 18, 1931 due to diabetic complications at his house in New Jersey, USA.

Quick Facts

- Edison was deaf and he liked it that way!

- He set up the world's first electric light power station in Lower Manhattan.

- Thomas Edison was famous for the following words, 'Genius is one percent inspiration, 99 percent perspiration'.

- He also invented the carbon microphone between the period, 1877-1878. This was used in all the telephones.

- His mother imparted him the basic education, teaching him reading, writing, and arithmetic. She also read to him from well-known English writers, such as Edward Gibbon, William Shakespeare, and Charles Dickens.

- Among his most important inventions were the electric light, the phonograph, and the motion-picture camera.

- The period from 1879 to 1900 is called the Age of Edison as this was the time span when he produced and perfected most of his devices.

Chapter - 13

S. CHANDRASEKHAR
(1910–1995)

S. Chandrasekhar or Subrahmanyan Chandrasekhar was an eminent Indian-American astrophysicist. He was honoured with a **Nobel Prize for Physics** in **1983**. He is world famous for giving the 'Chandrasekhar Limit'.

Biography

S. Chandrasekhar was born on October 19, 1910 in Lahore, Punjab. He was the nephew of Nobel laureate physicist Sir C. V. Raman. Initially tutored at home, Chandrasekhar attended the Hindu High School, Madras (Chennai) from 1922-25. From 1925-1930, he studied at the Presidency College, Chennai. In 1930, the Government of India awarded a scholarship to him for pursuing graduation in the University of Cambridge. He joined the Trinity College and in 1933, Chandrasekhar got his Ph.D. degree from Cambridge. He was elected to a prize fellowship at the university for four years (1933-1937).

Discoveries and Inventions

From 1929 to 1939, Chandrasekhar studied the stellar structure. From 1943 to 1950, he studied the theory of radiative transfer and the quantum theory of negative ion of hydrogen.

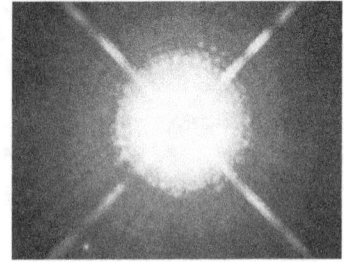

A White Dwarf Star

From 1950 to 1961, Chandrasekhar worked upon hydrodynamics and hydro genetic stability. He studied the mathematic theory of black holes from 1971 to 1983 and after that concentrated on the theory of colliding gravitational waves.

He is famous for his Chandrasekhar limit. It is defined as the maximum mass of a stable white dwarf star.

S. Chandrasekhar was awarded the Nobel Prize for Physics in 1983 for his studies on the physical processes important to the structure and evolution of stars. He was also honoured with the Padma Vibhushan in 1968.

S. Chandrasekhar died on August 21, 1995 in Chicago, USA.

Quick Facts

- A white dwarf star is a star which is about to extinguish in a few years. It is a final evolutionary stage of a star – beyond which it will not evolve.

- Chandrasekhar, known simply as "Chandra" in the scientific world, was one of ten children of Chandrasekhara Subrahmanyan Ayyar and Sitalakshmi Balakrishnan. Ayyar was an officer in the British government services. Sitalakshmi, a woman of great talent and self-taught intellectual attainments, played a pivotal role in her son's career.

- Chandrasekhar's uncle, Sir Chandrasekhara Venkata Raman was the recipient of a Nobel Prize for the celebrated discovery concerning the molecular scattering of light known as the "Raman Effect."

- He, too was awarded the Nobel Prize in Physics in 1983 for his studies on the physical processes important to the structure and evolution of stars. Chandrasekhar accepted this honour, but was upset that the citation mentioned only his earliest work, seeing it as a denigration of a lifetime's achievement. He shared it with William A. Fowler.

- Chandrasekhar was the managing editor of the Astrophysical Journal from 1952 to 1971. He converted essentially a private journal of the University of Chicago into a national journal of the American Astronomical Society.

Chapter - 14

DR. VIKRAM SARABHAI
(1919–1971)

Hailed as the Father of the Indian Space Program, Dr. Vikram Sarabhai was an eminent Indian physicist.

Biography

Born on August 12, 1919 in Ahmedabad, Gujarat as Vikram Ambalal Sarabhai, he was the son of a wealthy family. His father, Ambalal Sarabhai was a rich industrialist and owned many mills.

Vikram Sarabhai completed his secondary education from the Gujarat College, Ahmedabad after he passed his intermediate Science Examination. He next joined St. John's College, University of Cambridge, England. In 1940, he received the Tripos from the Cambridge University. He came back to India and joined the Indian Institute of Science, with the escalation of the World War II.

Discoveries and Inventions

At the Indian Institute of Science, Bangalore, presently called Bengaluru, Sarabhai started his research work in Cosmic Rays. He did his research under the guidance of his uncle, the eminent physicist, Sir C. V. Raman.

The Satellite, Aryabhata

He was offered a Doctor of Research Degree at the University of Cambridge for his thesis titled Cosmic Ray Investigation in Tropical Latitudes, in 1947. He had returned back to Cambridge in 1945 after the end of the war. In his thesis, he observed that there are immense opportunities opening up in solar as well as interplanetary physics.

Dr. Sarabhai returned to India after the Indian Independence. He played a significant role in establishing the Physical Research Laboratory in Ahmedabad in November, 1947. He also established many other educational institutions like the Indian Institute of Management (IIM), Centre for Environmental Planning and Technology (CEPT), Blind Men Association, etc.

Dr. Sarabhai set up the First Rocket Launching Setup (TERLS) in Thumba, Kerala with the help of Dr. Homi Jehangir Bhabha. The Satellite Instructional Television Experiment (SITE) was launched during 1975-76 as a result of his conversation with NASA in 1966. Aryabhatta, the first Indian satellite was put in orbit in 1975 as a result of Dr. Sarabhai`s project. He was very interested in science education and founded a Community Science Centre at Ahmedabad in 1966.

Vikram Sarabhai died on December 30, 1971 at Kovalam in Kerala.

Quick Facts

- Padma awards are the highest civilian awards of India.

- Vikram Sarabhai did research on the time variations of cosmic rays.

- He also visualised a new field of research opening up in Solar and was awarded `Dr. Shanti Swarup Bhatnagar Prize` in the year, 1962. He was conferred with the Padma Shri Award in 1966 and was awarded Padma Vibhushan in 1972.

- He was also appointed Chairman of the Atomic Energy Commission in May 1966 after the death of Dr. Homi Jehangir Bhabha.

- In the year, 1942, Vikram Sarabhai married Mrinalini Sarabhai, who was a famous classical dancer.

Chapter - 15

SIR JAGDISH CHANDRA BOSE
(1858–1937)

Sir or Acharya Jagadish Chandra Bose was an Indian physicist, biologist, botanist and archaeologist. He is well reputed for his contribution towards plant science and his research work in the field of radio and microwave optics. He is also well known for the invention of Crescograph. Dr. J. C. Bose was honoured with the title of 'Sir' after he was knighted in 1916 by the British government.

Biography

Dr. J. C. Bose was born on November 13, 1858 in Bikrampur, Bengal (now Bangladesh). He completed his primary education in a local school and then joined St. Xavier's School, Kolkata. He later got admission in St. Xavier's College, Kolkata. He then moved to England and got admission in Christ College, University of Cambridge to study natural sciences. In 1885, Bose returned to India and joined the Presidency College as the officiating professor of physics.

Discoveries and Inventions

Bose's most celebrated research was the discovery of the fact that plants respond to various stimuli. He demonstrated the response to stimulation between living and non-living.

His contribution in plant science is phenomenal. Through various experiments, he proved that plants grow faster with pleasant music and

Crescograph

gets stagnated amidst harsh sounds. He invented the **crescograph**, a device made to measure the growth in plants.

In the year 1894, Bose performed an experiment where he rang a bell at a distance using microwaves in millimetre length. He also made these microwaves ignite gunpowder.

His work on wireless communication found him an American patent and made him the first Indian to receive a patent from America. Bose is also regarded as the inventor of wireless telegraphy.

In 1895, Bose's first scientific paper titled 'On polarisation of electric rays by double refracting crystals' was communicated to the Asiatic Society of Bengal.

Sir J. C. Bose was also a writer. He is regarded as the first Bengali Science fiction writer. He wrote a science fiction piece of work named, 'Niruddesher Kahani' in Bengali in 1896.

Bose died on November 23, 1937.

- A stimulus or stimuli (plural) is an external substance or force which affects an activity.

- The year, 2008 was marked as the 150th birth anniversary of Sir Jagadish Chandra Bose who, at a relatively young age, established himself among the ranks of European scientists during the heyday of colonial rule in India.

- Bose's experiments were carried out at the Presidency College in Calcutta (Kolkata), although for demonstrations he developed a compact portable version of the equipment, including transmitter, receiver and various microwave components called the Bose's Apparatus. Some of his original equipment still exists, now at the Bose Institute in Kolkata.

Chapter - 16

SIR C. V. RAMAN
(1888–1970)

Sir C. V. Raman or Chandrasekhara Venkata Raman was an eminent **Indian physicist**. He was a **Nobel laureate** who received this coveted honour for his work titled the **'Raman effect'**.

Biography

Sir Chandrasekhara Venkata Raman was born in Thiruvanaikaval near Tiruchirappalli of Madras Presidency on November 7, 1888. Madras is presently known as Chennai. Raman moved to Andhra Pradesh to study in St. Aloysius Anglo-Indian High School at a very early age. At the age of 13, in 1902, Raman entered the Presidency College, Madras. He passed his Bachelor's in Physics with a gold medal in the year, 1904 and in 1907, Raman passed his Master's with distinction.

In 1917, Sir C. V. Raman took the Professorship in Physics at the University of Calcutta. Simultaneously, he continued his studies at the Indian Association for the Cultivation of Science. In 1934, he became the Director of the Indian **Institute of Science, Bangalore**, presently known as **Bengaluru**. Dr. C. V. Raman established a company called the Travancore Chemical and Manufacturing Company Ltd. in 1943 along with Dr. Krishnamurthy. He was conferred the British knighthood in the year 1929 and was thereafter known as Sir C. V. Raman.

Discoveries and Inventions

Sir C. V. Raman discovered the 'Raman effect' on February 28, 1928 while going through his experiment on the scattering of light.

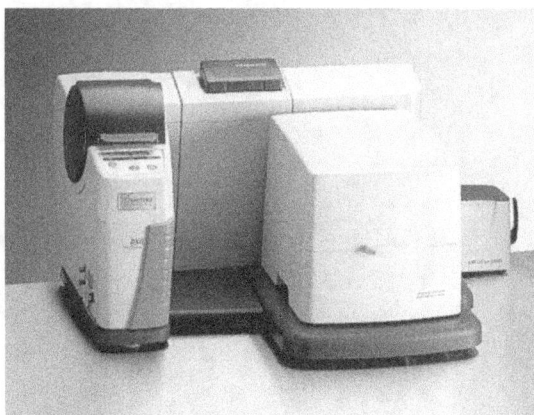

Raman's Spectrometer

Raman's Spectroscopy is a spectroscopic method used in physics and chemistry to study vibration, rotational and other low-frequency modes in a system.

He also worked on the traverse vibration of bow strings. He was the first one to investigate the harmonic sound of Indian instruments like tabla and mridanga.

Dr. C. V. Raman got worldwide reputation for his work in scattering of light and optics. In 1930, Sir C. V. Raman won the Nobel Prize for Physics for his work on scattering of light – the Raman Effect. He was also honoured with **Bharat Ratna** in **1954** and with the **Lenin Peace Prize** in the year **1957**.

Sir C. V. Raman died on November 21, 1970, aged 82.

Quick Facts

- Raman and Bhagavantam discovered the quantum photon spin in 1932, which further confirmed the quantum nature of light.

- Raman also worked on the acoustics of musical instruments.

- In 1948, Raman, through studying the spectroscopic behaviour of crystals, approached in a new manner fundamental problems of crystal dynamics. He also dealt with the structure and properties of diamond.

- India celebrates the National Science Day on February 28 of every year to commemorate the discovery of the Raman Effect in 1928.

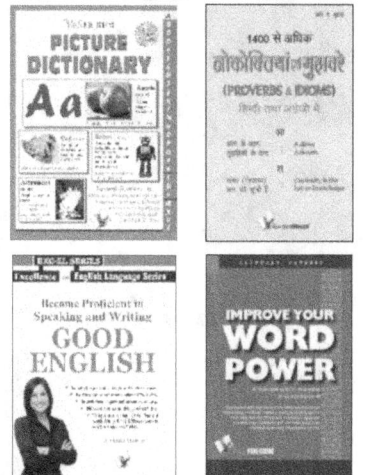

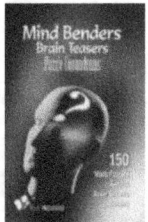

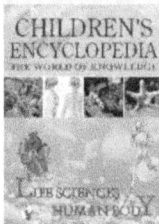

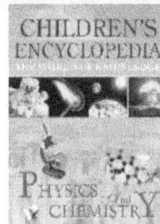

GENERAL HEALTH & BEAUTY CARE

MISCELLANEOUS

WATER
A Miracle Therapy

The Healing Power of MUDRAS
THE YOGA of the HANDS

Magneto Therapy
The miraculous healing remedy

Magic Therapy of COLOURS

एक्यूप्रेशर चिकित्सा

Reiki & Alternative Therapies

21 Power Foods of Reiki

FITNESS

मोटापा
कारण एवं निवारण

Stay Youthful Forever

योग और भोजन से रोगों का इलाज

Yogasanas & Pranayama

The Magic of Massage

Healing Power of MEDITATION

YOGASANAS and SADHANA
BESTSELLER

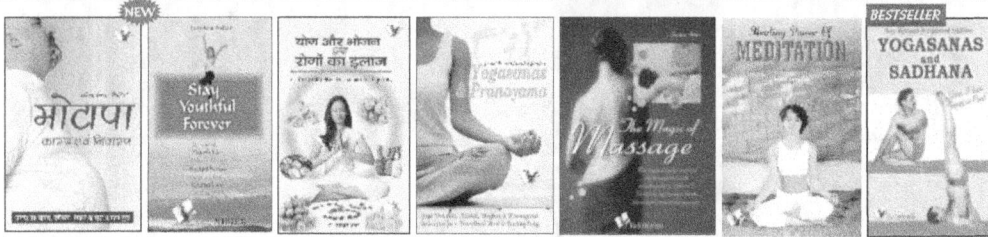

PERFECT HEALTH & AYURVEDA

FIT & FINE BODY & MIND

Ayurveda for All
BESTSELLER

NATURE CURE

सफल घरेलू इलाज

सर्वसुलभ जड़ी-बूटियों द्वारा रोगों का इलाज

KITCHEN CLINIC

PERFECT HEALTH
BODY DIET NUTRITION
BESTSELLER
A Set of 4 Books

DISEASES & COMMON AILMENTS

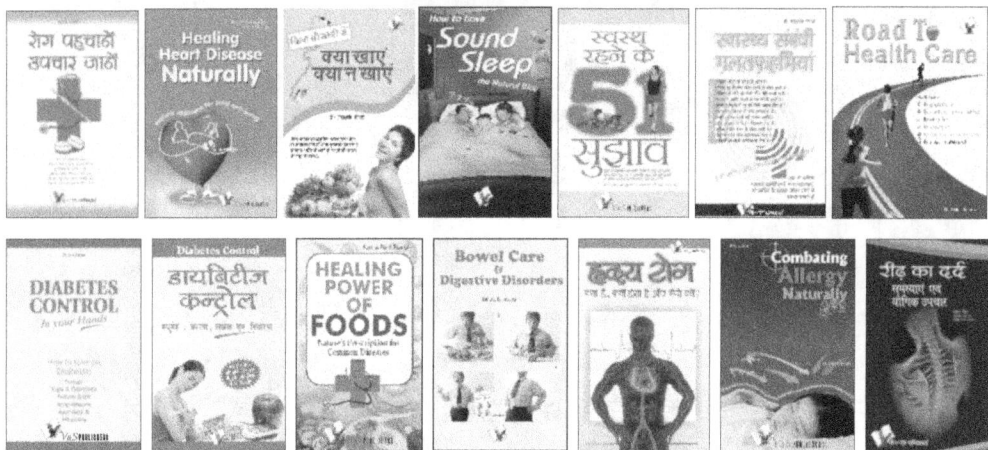

रोग पहचानो उपचार जानो

Healing Heart Disease Naturally

क्या खाएं क्या न खाएं

How to have Sound Sleep
the Natural Way

स्वस्थ रहने के 51 सुझाव

स्वास्थ्य संबंधी गलतफहमियां

Road To Health Care

DIABETES CONTROL
In your Hands

डायबिटीज कंट्रोल
Diabetes Control

HEALING POWER OF FOODS

Bowel Care & Digestive Disorders

हृदय रोग

Combating Allergy Naturally

रीढ़ का दर्द

REGIONAL LANGUAGE

तेलुगु-हिन्दी	हिन्दी-तेलुगु	ओड़िया-हिन्दी	हिन्दी-ओड़िया	मराठी-हिंदी	बांग्ला-हिंदी	हिन्दी-बांग्ला
(Telugu)		**(Odia)**		**(Marathi)**	**(Bangla)**	

AUTISM

क्या है

मातृकला

होम्योपैथी चिकित्सा

CONCISE DICTIONARY OF PLACEMENTS

बॉडी लैंग्वेज

SPOKEN ENGLISH

SPOKEN ENGLISH

SPOKEN ENGLISH

SPOKEN ENGLISH